WHO ARE THE DOLPHINS?

The Miami Dolphins are a team in the National Football League (NFL). They are one of the 32 teams in the NFL. The NFL includes the American Football Conference (AFC) and the National Football Conference (NFC). The winner of the AFC plays the winner of the NFC in the **Super Bowl**. The Dolphins play in the East Division of the AFC. They have won two Super Bowls.

Quarterback Ryan Tannehill passes the ball against the Buffalo Bills on September 14, 2014.

WHERE THEY CAME FROM

The Dolphins joined the American Football League (AFL) in 1966. They played in a stadium called the Orange Bowl. The Dolphins and the other AFL teams joined the NFL in 1970. The Dolphins also hired coach Don Shula that year. They were great under Shula. The team made it to three Super Bowls in a row. They won all their games in 1972, including the Super Bowl. It is the only perfect season in NFL history. The Dolphins moved to a new stadium in 1987. They still play there today.

Dolphins players carry coach Don Shula off of the field on January 14, 1973. The Dolphins beat the Washington Redskins to finish a perfect season.

WHO THEY PLAY

The Miami Dolphins play 16 games each season. With so few games, every one is important. Each year, the Dolphins play two games against each of the other three teams in their division: the Buffalo Bills, the New England Patriots, and the New York Jets. The Dolphins and the Jets are big **rivals**. They have played many exciting games against each other.

The Dolphins and Jets play hard against each other no matter what the standings say.

WHERE THEY PLAY

The Dolphins play at Sun Life Stadium. The stadium seats more than 75,000 fans. It is shaped like a rectangle. This allows baseball and soccer teams to play there, too. Baseball's Florida Marlins played there from 1993 to 2011. Miami has hosted ten Super Bowls. The Orange Bowl hosted five. Sun Life Stadium has hosted five more. Only New Orleans has hosted as many Super Bowls.

Circular ramps help people get to their seats at Sun Life Stadium.

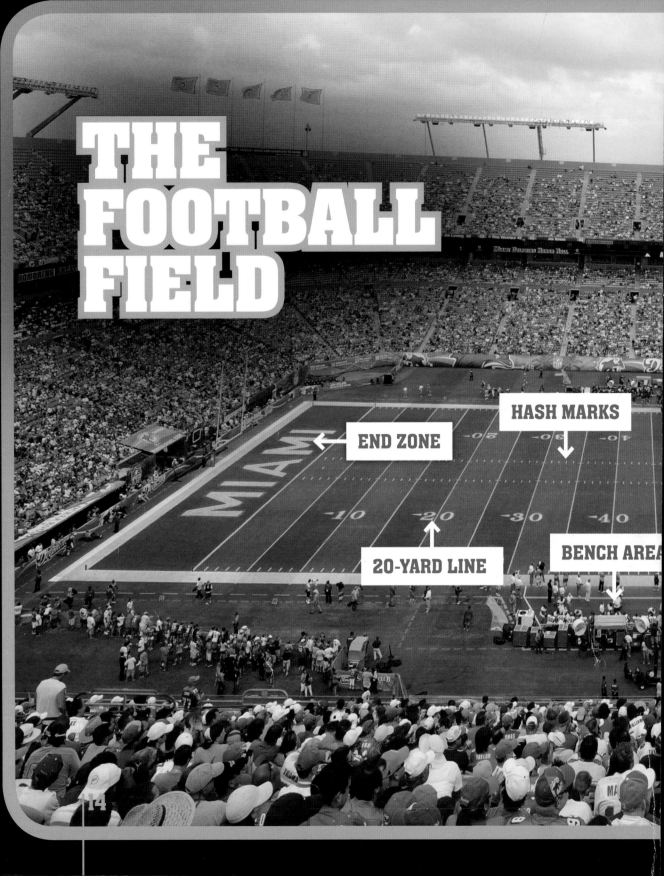

THE FOOTBALL FIELD

END ZONE

HASH MARKS

20-YARD LINE

BENCH AREA

14

SIDELINE

GOAL POST

MIDFIELD

GOAL LINE

END LINE

BIG DAYS

The Dolphins have had some great moments in their history. Here are three of the greatest:

1972—The Dolphins won all 14 games in the regular season. They beat the Cleveland Browns and the Pittsburgh Steelers in the playoffs. Then they won the Super Bowl 14-7 over the Washington Redskins. No other team has won all of its games in a year including the Super Bowl.

1973—The Dolphins had another great season after their perfect one. They lost only two games. They beat the Minnesota Vikings 24-7 in the Super Bowl on January 13, 1974. It was the Dolphins' third straight Super Bowl appearance. It was their second straight Super Bowl win.

Quarterback Bob Griese hands the ball off to fullback Larry Csonka in the Super Bowl on January 13, 1974.

1993—The Dolphins beat the Philadelphia Eagles 19-14 on November 14. It was Don Shula's 325th win. It made him the coach with the most wins in NFL history.

TOUGH DAYS

Football is a hard game. Even the best teams have rough games and seasons. Here are some of the toughest times in Dolphins history:

1975—Star running backs Larry Csonka and Jim Kiick and receiver Paul Warfield left the Dolphins. They went to play in the new World Football League. The Dolphins went 10-4. But they missed the playoffs for the first time since 1969.

1993—Dolphins quarterback Dan Marino was in the prime of his career. But he got hurt in the fifth game of the season. He did not play for the rest of the year. The Dolphins finished 9-7. They missed the playoffs.

A trainer checks out quarterback Dan Marino's injured leg on the sideline on October 10, 1993. Marino did not play the rest of the season because of the injury.

2007—Miami went 1-15 in Cam Cameron's only year as coach. They scored only 267 points. They allowed 437.

MEET THE FANS

There are many other outdoor things for people to do in South Florida. But Dolphins fans always show up to cheer on their team. On sunny days, they **tailgate** outside the stadium before the game. Mascot T.D. gets fans excited for the team during the game. A real dolphin swam behind the end zone from 1966 to 1968. It would jump in the air when the home team scored.

A young fan and her mother arrive early to tailgate outside Sun Life Stadium.

HEROES THEN

Dan Marino is one of the best quarterbacks in football history. Marino set records for touchdown passes, passing yards, and completions. He made nine **Pro Bowls**. He retired in 1999 after 17 seasons. And he entered the Pro Football **Hall of Fame** in 2005. Coach Don Shula is also in the Hall of Fame. He had only two losing seasons in 26 years with the Dolphins. Fullback Larry Csonka was one of Shula's top players. He is also in the Hall of Fame. He was big and hard to tackle. Csonka scored 68 touchdowns in his career. He fumbled only 21 times. Quarterback Bob Griese, receiver Paul Warfield, and center Jim Langer were also stars. They helped the Dolphins win their two Super Bowls.

Quarterback Dan Marino gets set to pass in a game against the San Diego Chargers on January 8, 1995.

HEROES NOW

Today, the Dolphins are a young team trying to prove it can win championships. Quarterback Ryan Tannehill was picked in the first round of the 2012 **NFL Draft**. He has a strong arm, moves well, and makes smart decisions. Mike Pouncey is considered one of the league's best offensive linemen. On defense, Brent Grimes is a top cornerback. He had nine interceptions in his first two seasons with the Dolphins. Defensive tackle Ndamukong Suh and defensive end Cameron Wake are both top pass-rushers.

Cornerback Brent Grimes stretches to intercept a ball in a game against the Detroit Lions on November 9, 2014.

GEARING UP

NFL players wear team uniforms. They wear helmets and pads to keep them safe. Cleats help them make quick moves and run fast. Some players wear extra gear for protection.

THE FOOTBALL

NFL footballs are made of leather. Under the leather is a lining that fills with air to give the ball its shape. The leather has bumps, or "pebbles." These help players grip the ball. Laces help players control their throws. Footballs are also called "pigskins" because some of the first balls were made from pig bladders. Today, they are made of leather from cows.

Running back Lamar Miller speeds past a Denver Broncos defender on November 23, 2014.

HELMET

SHOULDER PADS

GLOVES

THIGH PADS

FOOTBALL

CLEATS

SPORTS STATS

Here are some of the all-time career records for the Miami Dolphins. All the stats are through the 2014 season.

RUSHING YARDS

Larry Csonka 6,737

Ricky Williams 6,436

PASSING YARDS

Dan Marino 61,361

Bob Griese 25,092

TOTAL TOUCHDOWNS

Mark Clayton 82

Nat Moore 75

INTERCEPTIONS

Jake Scott 35

Dick Anderson 34

RECEPTIONS

Mark Clayton 550

Mark Duper 511

POINTS

Olindo Mare 1,048

Garo Yepremian 830

Defensive end Cameron Wake sacks New England Patriots quarterback Tom Brady on September 7, 2014. Wake has been to four Pro Bowls.

SACKS

Jason Taylor 131

Cameron Wake 63

GLOSSARY

expansion when a league grows by adding a team or teams

Hall of Fame a museum in Canton, Ohio, that honors the best players in NFL history

NFL Draft a meeting of all the NFL teams at which they choose college players to join them

Pro Bowls NFL all-star games, in which the best players in the league compete

rivals teams whose games bring out the greatest emotion between the players and the fans on both sides

Super Bowl the championship game of the NFL, played between the winner of the AFC and the NFC

tailgate when fans gather outside of the stadium before a game to picnic around their vehicles

touchdown a play in which the ball is held in the other team's end zone, resulting in six points

FIND OUT MORE

IN THE LIBRARY

Frisch, Aaron. *Miami Dolphins.*
San Francisco: Chronicle Books, 2014.

Wilcox, Billy G., III. *Dolphinology Trivia Challenge.*
Lewis Center, OH: Kick The Ball, 2011.

Wyner, Zach. *Miami Dolphins.* New York:
Av2 by Weigl, 2014.

ON THE WEB

Visit our Web site for links about the Miami Dolphins:
childsworld.com/links

Note to Parents, Teachers, and Librarians: We routinely verify our Web links to make sure they are safe and active sites. So encourage your readers to check them out!

INDEX